TERRORIST ATTACKS

THE CRASH OF UNITED FLIGHT 93 ON SEPTEMBER 11, 2001

Tonya Buell

The Rosen Publishing Group, Inc.
New York

To the late Michael Theodoridis, my friend and mentor, who was killed in the crash of American Airlines Flight 11 on the morning of September 11, 2001.

Published in 2003 by The Rosen Publishing Group, Inc.
29 East 21st Street, New York, NY 10010

First Edition

Library of Congress Cataloging-in-Publication Data

Buell, Tonya.
The crash of United Flight 93 on September 11, 2001/by Tonya Buell.—1st ed.
        p. cm—(Terrorist attacks)
Summary: An account of the events surrounding the hijacking and crash of United Flight 93 as part of the terrorist plot carried out on September 11, 2001. Includes bibliographical references and index.
ISBN 0-8239-3857-3 (library binding)
1. United Airlines Flight 93 Hijacking Incident, 2001—Juvenile literature.
2. Hijacking of aircraft—United States—Juvenile literature. 3. Terrorism—United States—Juvenile literature. [1. United Airlines Flight 93 Hijacking Incident, 2001. 2. Hijacking of aircraft. 3. Terrorism.]
I. Title. II. Series.
HV6432 .B84 2003
974.8'79044—dc21

                                                                2002010244

Manufactured in the United States of America

CONTENTS

INTRODUCTION

On the morning of September 11, 2001, four planes were hijacked by radical terrorists. Each of the planes crashed, killing all of the people on board. Three of the planes crashed into important and populous American landmarks: one into each of the twin towers of the World Trade Center in New York City, and one into the Pentagon outside Washington, D.C. The fourth plane, United Airlines Flight 93, crashed into a rural field in Pennsylvania. This plane became the subject of intense investigation because, unlike the others, it didn't crash into a well-known structure. What happened on United Airlines Flight 93 that made its fate differ from the other three planes that were hijacked that day? Why did it crash into a wooded field instead of an important building filled with innocent people?

The true story of the hijacking of United Airlines Flight 93 is more a series of questions than answers. We know that several terrorists aboard the plane took control of it, but why? We know that the airplane crashed in a field in Pennsylvania on that fateful morning, but what happened inside the plane before it crashed? We know that three other planes were also hijacked that same morning, all by the

On September 11, 2001, United Airlines Flight 93, bound for San Francisco, California, from Newark, New Jersey, crashed into a field near Shanksville, Pennsylvania, after an attempted hijacking. The crash burned trees and created this large crater. All forty passengers and crew, as well as the four hijackers, were killed.

same group of terrorists. But what did this group hope to accomplish by killing so many innocent civilians?

After examining the details of this tragic tale, federal authorities have been able to reach a number of reasonable conclusions. But much is still left uncertain. What exactly happened inside the airplane after it was hijacked? Who was injured or killed early on, and who fought back? What would have happened if the passengers had been able to gain control of the airplane before it crashed?

In this book, we examine the facts and evidence surrounding the hijacking of United Airlines Flight 93 and attempt to make some sense of the tragedy that occurred on that late summer morning.

FBI agents search the crash site of United Airlines Flight 93. After a plane crash, government officials examine any debris from the crash for clues, and search for the plane's voice recorder and "black box."

EVIL IN THE NAME OF GOOD

Islam is a religion practiced by millions of people throughout the world. People who practice Islam are called Muslims. Islam was founded by the prophet Muhammad in the city of Mecca in Saudi Arabia over a thousand years ago. The holy book of Islam is called the Koran, and Muslims call God "Allah."

Like most religions, Islam teaches its members to be peaceful, loving, and kind to others. There are five main teachings that Muslims are supposed to follow. First is the profession of faith, or stating that one believes in Allah. Second is prayer. Third is almsgiving, or

Mecca is a city in Saudi Arabia considered sacred to many Muslims. The K'abah, shown here, is a square building inside a mosque in the center of Mecca. Once a year, millions of Muslims visit Mecca to perform the hajj ceremony.

charitable giving to the poor. Fourth is fasting, or going without food for a period of time, and fifth is a journey to Mecca, the city where Islam originated. Islam does not teach its members to be mean or hateful to others, and it does not teach its members to kill innocent people. But there are times, as we saw on September 11, 2001, when people practice evil in the name of good.

Misinterpreting a Religion

Religions and their holy books are subject to interpretation. One group of people may think that what the holy book of its religion says means one thing, while another group will believe that it means something entirely different. This is true for almost every religion.

Some people believe their holy books should be interpreted literally, or word for word, while others think that the books should be interpreted symbolically. Some people think that their religion is right and all other religions are wrong. This causes certain people to believe that they are right and good, and that people who don't believe as they do are wrong and bad. Of course, this is not true. Everyone in the world, no matter what he or she believes, has a chance to live his or her life in a positive manner by being good, kind, and caring to others.

When people begin to believe that they are good and that everyone else is bad, they may use their interpretation of their religion to cause harm to those who do not believe as they do. People who act in this way are usually called extremists or fanatics.

Most people understand that their religion, whatever religion it may be, teaches peace and kindness. But there are times when people in the world misinterpret their religion and believe that it teaches them to cause harm to those who they think are bad. They may believe that they are doing good by attempting to force their ideas and their religion on those who believe differently, but in truth they are merely acting against their own religion's belief system.

A Network of Terror

The group of people who committed the hijackings and terrorist acts on September 11 were among those who are widely considered to have misinterpreted their religion. This group, started by a man named Osama bin Laden, is called Al Qaeda. Al Qaeda teaches its members that all people in the world who do not follow Al Qaeda's belief system are evil.

The Al Qaeda organization has committed many terrorist acts. Its members believe that the acts they commit are actually for the good and betterment of their community and the world. Terrorism is the act of hurting or trying to hurt innocent people in an attempt to gain the political or religious goals of a group or individual. A terrorist is one who practices or believes in terrorism. Al Qaeda is a group of terrorists. Instead of working with governments and religious groups and discussing their ideas and beliefs peacefully, they use bombs and other weapons to hurt innocent people. They hope that the people with whom they disagree will succumb to their ideas out of fear.

Al Qaeda is a large organization, with members scattered throughout the world. It entices young, vulnerable Muslims to join the organization, and it teaches ideas of evil and terror to these young people. Since the horrible destruction that was committed on September 11 by members of this group, the United States and many other nations have attempted to stop Al Qaeda from growing and

ISLAM AND THE REAL MEANING OF JIHAD

Many Americans and people of other Western nations may come to the conclusion that, because a handful of Muslims carried out horrible acts of terror, all Muslims are evil or bad. But this is not true. Islam is a peaceful religion, and most Muslims were as shocked and horrified by the tragedy on September 11 as members of other religions were.

Islamic terrorist groups use the concept of jihad as an excuse for their crimes. Jihad is a word described in Islam's holy book, the Koran, and means "to struggle." Islamic terrorists interpret this to mean to fight or wage a holy war with others who don't follow their belief system. But this is not what the meaning of jihad is at all.

Most Muslims believe that jihad refers to one's struggle in life, the struggle to become a better person or a better Muslim. Jihad can be interpreted to mean an intellectual, spiritual, social, moral, or political struggle. For example, a Muslim may consider his or her personal struggle to become a better person and to live a better life as a jihad.

The Koran and Islamic laws strictly forbid suicide, the killing of women and children, and the killing or hurting of anyone when not first attacked. All of these rules are broken by terrorists who commit harmful acts against others, and therefore these terrorists are not true to the Muslim faith. Most Muslims are appalled at the terrorist acts that are committed. They don't want others to consider them bad people just because they are Muslim.

committing any more acts of terror. However, that is not so easy because there are many members of this organization scattered around the globe.

Al Qaeda had committed numerous other acts of terrorism before September 11, and the governments of the United States and other nations worked to stop their acts of terrorism long before then. Since September 11, however, when the United States and other nations saw the high degree of destruction that could be committed by this and other terrorist groups, they have worked much harder to stop Al Qaeda and to stamp out all terrorist organizations.

Preparations

For several years before September 11, 2001, the members of Al Qaeda prepared for the terrorist acts that they were to commit. Prior to the retaliations from the United States and other nations after September 11, Al Qaeda had control of massive training camps in Afghanistan. There, Al Qaeda members learned how to act, how to go undetected, and how to fight when carrying out a terrorist mission.

Many of the terrorists who committed the hijackings on September 11 moved to America long before the event, living in hotels and rented apartments, trying to fit in while at the same time preparing for their terrorist missions. They were taught to fit in with Americans so that they would not look suspicious. They were often quiet and did not interact with their neighbors so that no one would know who they were. They shaved their beards, which are often worn by Muslims, and they dressed in Western clothing. They were hiding in plain sight.

T 186—Apartment lease. 2-5 family dwelling
plain English format. 3-88

PREPARED BY ARNOLD MANDELL, L.L.B.

© 1978 BY JULIUS BLUMBERG, INC.,
PUBLISHER, NYC 10013

LEASE AGREEMENT

The Landlord and Tenant agree to lease the Apartment at the Rent and for the Term stated on these terms:

LANDLORD: _Henry Mazur_   TENANT: _Mr. Ziad Jarrah_ / _Hassan Jarrah_

Address for Notices: _315 E 3 ST._   _315 — E 3 ST_

Bklyn N.Y. 11218   _Bklyn N Y 11218_

Apartment (and terrace, if any) .... at .... _2 Floor   3 Bed Room Apt_

| Lease date: _March 1_ 1995 | Term beginning _March 1_ — 1995
ending _Feb 28_, 1996 | Yearly Rent $ _9600.00_
Monthly Rent $ _800.00_
Security $ _800.00_ |

Rider   Additional terms on .... page(s) initialed at the end by the parties is attached and made a part of this Lease.

1. Use
     The Apartment must be used only as a private Apartment to live in and for no other reason. Only a party signing this Lease and the spouse and children of that party may use the Apartment.

2. Failure to give possession
     Landlord shall not be liable for failure to give Tenant possession of the Apartment on the beginning date of the Term. Rent shall be payable as of the beginning of the Term unless Landlord is unable to give possession. Rent shall then be payable as of the date possession is available. Landlord will notify Tenant as to the date possession is available. The ending date of the Term will not change.

This document shows that in 1995, Ziad M. Jarrah, believed to be one of the hijackers of Flight 93, leased an apartment in Brooklyn, New York. The September 11 terrorists lived virtually undetected in many American cities.

One of their main objectives before the hijackings was to learn how to fly commercial jet airplanes. Several of the terrorists enrolled in flight training schools, and some were seen by neighbors practicing flying commercial airplanes on computer flight simulators in their homes. Their neighbors stated that all they seemed to do all day long was practice on the flight simulators.

Finally, the terrorists determined that they were ready. The date was set, and their preparations were complete. We don't know how much each of the individual terrorists knew about what was to happen. They knew that they had been taught to fit in, that they had learned the skill of flying a commercial jet airplane, and that they each knew to which city and airport to report.

While investigators continue to search for clues, an American flag waves over an altar constructed near the crash site of United Airlines Flight 93.

A SERIES OF MISHAPS

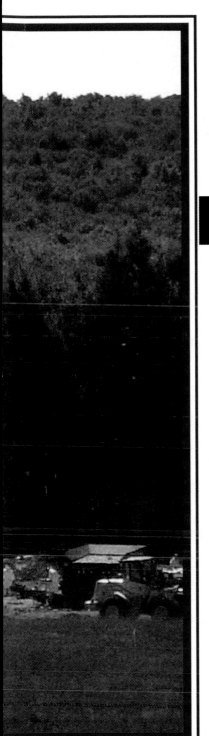

To hijack an airplane is to take it over by force, usually with the use of weapons or the threat of a bomb. The hijackers then force the pilots of the airplane to fly the plane to a different destination than was originally intended. In the past, most hijacked planes were landed at different airports than their original intended destination.

On the morning of September 11, 2001, terrorists gave new meaning to the word hijacking. Instead of forcing the pilots of the airplanes to fly the planes to different destinations, the terrorists killed or injured the pilots and took over the controls of the airplanes themselves. The hijackers then crashed the planes into important and populated American buildings. Two of these planes, American Airlines Flight 11 and United Airlines Flight 175, slammed into the twin towers of New York City's World Trade Center. Another airplane, American Airlines Flight 77, crashed into the Pentagon building outside of Washington, D.C. One can only assume that a similar fate was destined for United Airlines Flight 93.

The plans were all set. The hijackers had been preparing for years for this moment. But United Airlines Flight 93 was the only plane in which the hijackers' plans were not carried out. What went wrong? What stopped the terrorists from carrying out their evil plan?

A number of things stopped them. First, they seemed to be one short of the five hijackers that the other planes carried. In addition, their plane was delayed for over forty minutes, sitting on the runway of an overcrowded airport. Finally, the terrorists who hijacked United Airlines Flight 93 most certainly didn't expect the bravery of the passengers and crew on the airplane. From the very beginning, before the plane even left the ground, and before the fateful day began, there was a series of mishaps.

The Missing Hijacker

The three other airplanes that were hijacked that day each contained five hijackers. The terrorists are believed to have planned for each of the four planes to contain five hijackers, enough to kill or wound the pilots, take control of the airplanes, and guard the passengers so that the terrorists would be able to carry out their horrible tasks. However, United Airlines Flight 93 only carried four hijackers. What had happened to the fifth?

Investigators believe that Zacarias Moussaoui was intended to be the fifth hijacker on United Airlines Flight 93. Unfortunately for the terrorists,

Zacarias Moussaoui was the only person charged in the September 11, 2001, attacks. Government officials believe that if he had not already been under arrest for an expired visa on September 11, he would have been the fifth hijacker on United Airlines Flight 93.

he wasn't around when the time came to hijack the airplanes. A few months earlier, at Pan Am Flying Academy in Eagen, Minnesota, Moussaoui asked to be trained to fly a commercial jet airplane.

Instructors at the flight academy immediately became suspicious. Moussaoui had only fifty-five hours of flying time in a small training plane, but wanted to learn to fly a commercial craft. According to the Guardian Unlimited Web site, he had e-mailed the academy that he wanted ". . . to be able to pilot one of these Big Bird [*sic*], even if I am not a real professional pilot." Along with the significant amount of pilot training Moussaoui was requesting, he paid the academy not with a check or credit card, but with a bundle of cash. After careful thought, the instructors at the flight academy decided to alert the Federal Bureau of Investigation (FBI).

The FBI investigated Moussaoui. They asked his neighbors about him, performed a background check, and checked his immigration status. Although he was quiet and polite but not outgoing or friendly with the neighbors, the FBI was able to learn that he had recently purchased pilot training videos. They also discovered that he was on a wanted terrorist list, and that his U.S. visa had expired. The FBI immediately arrested Moussaoui and held him on immigration charges.

Apparently, the terrorist organization that planned the horrific deeds on September 11 wasn't able to find anyone to replace Moussaoui. They most likely didn't plan on his detainment, especially after he had been in the United States for so long without having any problems. Whatever the reason, United Airlines Flight 93 left the ground on the morning of September 11, 2001, with only four hijackers.

Delays

United Airlines Flight 93 was scheduled to leave Newark, New Jersey, for San Francisco, California, at 8:01 AM on

September 11. The terrorists had timed the four flights that they were planning to hijack so that all of the flights would take off at almost exactly the same time. This way, they would be able to carry out their evil plans before local or federal authorities could be alerted and before anyone could take measures to stop them. As soon as each plane was in the air, they planned to take over the airplane, turn it around, and crash it into one of several important U.S. buildings and landmarks, all at approximately the same time.

However, the runway at the crowded airport in Newark was busy that morning, and although the plane, along with its passengers and crew, pulled away from the gate at 8:01 AM, it sat on the runway. The terrorists were seated in first class, and both the passengers and the terrorists sat back in their seats, waiting for the plane to take off. Finally, forty-one minutes later, at 8:42 AM, the plane was given permission by Newark's air traffic control center to take off.

About twenty minutes after the plane took off, the pilots received a notice of warning. By that time, American Airlines Flight 11 had already crashed into the first tower of the World Trade Center, and United Airlines Flight 175 was only minutes away from the second tower. "Beware, cockpit intrusion," warned air traffic control on the computer screen in the airplane's cockpit. The United Airlines pilots took note of the warning and responded confidently, "Confirmed."

Passengers settled down in their seats while the flight attendants served them their morning meal. On each of the other three planes that were hijacked that day, the terrorists took control of the plane right away, just after the plane was in the air and headed toward its destination. But on United Airlines Flight 93, the terrorists had their breakfast and first-class service along with the other passengers. Instead of rushing into the cockpit to take control of the plane immediately, as the terrorists did in the other three hijacked planes, the terrorists on United Airlines Flight 93 waited. No one knows why. Perhaps they were comfortable, tired, or overly confident in their ability to carry out their mission. However, we do know this: Their tardiness, in the end, proved to be an important mistake.

Bonding Between the Passengers

Finally, at about 9:25 AM, fifteen minutes after both of the World Trade Center towers had been hit by two of the other hijacked airplanes, and about fifteen minutes before the Pentagon was to be hit by the third airplane, the terrorists on United Airlines Flight 93 decided to make their move. Passengers in first class watched curiously as those whom they assumed to be innocent passengers like themselves tied red bandannas around their heads. The men then stood up, rushed into the cockpit, and began struggling with the pilots. "Hey, get out of here!" one of the pilots shouted, a shout that was heard by the air traffic control center on the ground.

On September 11, 2001, smoke poured from both towers of the World Trade Center in New York City after they were each hit by a hijacked plane. Shortly after this photo was taken, both towers collapsed.

Captain Jason Dahl, the main pilot, had learned to fly before he could even drive. He and his copilot, Leroy Homer, attempted to fight back, alerting air traffic controllers with the sounds of their shouting and the scuffle that occurred between the pilots and the terrorists. Unfortunately, they were not successful. Eventually, the pilots were overtaken and the terrorists took control of the airplane.

After gaining control of the airplane, the terrorists turned it around and signified a change in plans to air traffic control. They asked air traffic control for a new destination: Washington, D.C.

The terrorists rounded up the terrified passengers and flight attendants on the airplane and forced them to

A VOICE HEARD OVER THE AIRWAVES

Air traffic controllers couldn't believe what they were hearing. "This is the captain speaking," came a thickly accented voice through the airwaves to the air traffic control center in Cleveland, Ohio. "Remain in your seat. There is a bomb on board. Stay quiet. We are meeting with their demands. We are returning to the airport."

Clearly, this message was meant to be directed to the passengers of United Airlines Flight 93, not the local air traffic controllers. Had the hijackers flipped the wrong switch? It is possible that one of the pilots may have flipped the communications switch to air traffic control during their struggle with the terrorists, and that the terrorists had, in their haste, not turned it off. Regardless of what exactly happened, the hijackers instantly realized their mistake, and that they were speaking with airline officials, not to their captive passengers as they had intended. The hijackers became flustered, flipping several switches on and off and shouting at one another until they finally turned off the microphone to air traffic control.

They were clearly upset that their statement had been made to the wrong group of people—air traffic controllers who could easily alert the authorities, instead of the captive passengers and crew. It is also clear that they were rather unfamiliar with the controls in the cockpit. It is not known, however, if the passengers of United Airlines Flight 93 ever even heard the message.

move to the last five rows of the airplane, rows thirty to thirty-four. The passengers and flight attendants were guarded by just one hijacker, a man in his early twenties who had a red box around his waist. He claimed it was a bomb. Moving the passengers and flight attendants to the back of the airplane proved to be another crucial mistake. Formerly strangers, the passengers instantly bonded, talking with one another and discussing their terrifying situation. They talked about their families and discussed their various skills and options.

The terrorist who was supposed to be guarding the passengers apparently did not seem to be very threatening. He may have even left the passengers alone for some time. Whatever the case, the passengers felt free enough to talk among themselves, to discuss what was happening, and to make telephone calls from their cell phones as well as from Airphones, the telephones located on the backs of the seats in each row of the airplane. They instantly began calling their loved ones to tell them what was happening, to find out what was going on throughout the rest of the United States, or simply to express their love.

UNITED

Tuesday S...

SFO Update

Due to the events on the East Coast.
All arrivals into San Francisco Internation...
have been suspened or diverted to other
cities.
This will resulted in numerous
delays and/or cancellations. We will upd...
the public monitors with information as ...
becomes available.
For more information, please call:

1 800 241 6522

Monitors at San Francisco International Airport on September 11, 2001, announce the cancellation of all flights into or out of San Francisco.

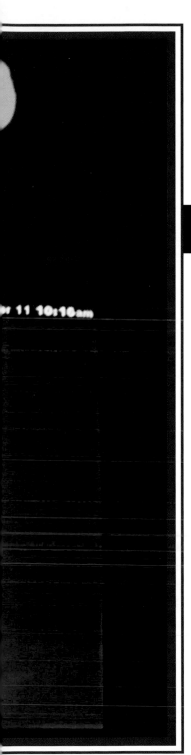

HEROES, NOT VICTIMS

CHAPTER 3

At first glance, one would think that the passengers of this doomed flight were helpless victims of the terrorist organization's evil plot. Their plane was hijacked, taken over by four terrorists who claimed they had a bomb and who had turned the plane around toward an unknown destination. They were hostages in an airplane flying 30,000 feet above the ground. Trapped in this large metal cage, it may appear that they had no chance of survival, much less of working out a plan or a means to overpower the terrorists.

The passengers and remaining crew must have been

terrified and in complete shock. What they had initially expected to be a routine flight across the country had turned into terror in the sky. Who could be expected to do more than tremble at the fate that they were facing? What would you do, if you were faced with a similar situation?

Most people might shiver in fear or plead for their lives. In a situation such as this, many people would cry, pray, or do anything to calm their fears. However, as we take a closer look at the situation that occurred, and as we examine the passengers who were on board the plane that day, we can see that the passengers were actually heroes, not victims.

The Wrong Plane to Attack

United Airlines Flight 93 was, by all accounts, the wrong plane to attack. In the terrorists' eyes, the passengers may have appeared to be a small mix of women, disabled people, and the elderly, with a few men among them. However, the passengers and crew of this plane were actually a fierce blend of activists, former law enforcement officers, martial arts experts, athletes, and airplane and flight experts.

One of the flight attendants had worked for United Airlines for thirty-seven years and was very familiar with the airline's and the government's flight emergency procedures. Another had been a flight attendant for more than twenty-five years and was also well-versed in how to handle emergency situations. Yet another had once been a police detective and had trained and worked with the police force in Florida for years. She had only recently decided to change her career to live out her dream of becoming a flight attendant.

Among the passengers was a 6'3" rock climber who was formerly a prosecutor for Scotland Yard, England's police headquarters. In first class sat a 6'4" rugby player, who had once fought off an armed mugger carrying a gun. Across the aisle from him sat a former college quarterback. One of the passengers was 6'2", weighed 220 pounds, and was a recognized judo champion. One woman held a brown belt in karate.

One of the passengers was a weight lifter who sported a Superman tattoo on his forearm. Another was a law enforcement officer with the California Fish and Wildlife Department who had been trained in hand-to-hand combat. One passenger, a retired ironworker, had been in the military in his younger years and remained in very good shape. One was a single-engine aircraft pilot who knew anything and everything about airplanes, according to his family. Another was a former air traffic controller with the Air National Guard.

There were a couple of missionaries, who would know how to produce calm in the most frightening of situations. There was a tiny woman who walked with a cane and appeared meek at first glance, but who was actually a powerful activist for the disabled. There was a 6'1", 200-pound

A memorial poster for student Deora Bodley, a passenger on United Airlines Flight 93, on the University of California Santa Clara campus.

Cathy Stefani, mother of Flight 93 passenger Nicole Carole Miller, holds a picture of her daughter. At left is Nicole's older sister, Tiffney Miller.

Kevin Marisay, the brother of passenger Georgine Corrigan, holds a memorial poster for her as he prepares to listen to the flight recorder tape with other passengers' families.

football player, an avid baseball fan, and several business executives. The list goes on and on.

These were people who, on their own, would each be able to handle a crisis situation. Together, they formed a team that was almost invincible. This was not a group to contend with.

Phone Calls and Final Good-byes

As the hijackers scrambled to turn the plane around and head toward Washington, D.C., the passengers and crew at the back of the plane used Airphones and cell phones to call their families and loved ones. Husbands called wives and wives called husbands, sending them final words of love and asking about the situation in other areas of the nation. Sons called mothers, sisters called sisters, and friends called friends.

Some of the passengers made more than one telephone call, and some remained on the phone for a very long time. Through these telephone calls, the passengers learned of the plane crashes into the two World Trade Center towers and into the Pentagon. They traded stories with one another, confirming accounts given to them by their loved ones. One man asked his wife to call the FBI, while another passenger dialed 911. A few of the passengers asked their loved ones if the stories that they had heard from their fellow passengers, about other planes crashing into the World Trade Center towers and the

Pentagon, were in fact true. Some tried to tell their friends on the ground approximately where they were located so that law enforcement officials could be notified.

The passengers made a total of twenty-three phone calls from the Airphones on the plane, and many more were made from personal cell phones. A passenger would call his or her loved one, say a few words and then pass the phone to another passenger, allowing that person to make a call. Those who owned cellular telephones lent their phones to the passengers seated next to them. A tremendous amount of camaraderie and teamwork built up among these courageous passengers.

As the passengers made more and more phone calls and traded their stories with one another, they began to realize that their plane was destined to crash into a major landmark, like the others, killing not only themselves but potentially hundreds or even thousands more innocent people on the ground. They began to realize that they were doomed to die unless they did something about it. They also realized that many, many other innocent people might die as well if they did not take action.

The Vote

As the passengers became more aware of their situation, they realized that their only option was to take action. They came to understand that, instead of sitting back and obeying the hijackers' demands, as was common practice in airline

AN IMPORTANT PHONE CALL

Something was wrong. Todd Beamer was attempting to contact his wife, Lisa, on one of the airplane's Airphones, but he could not get through. He was redirected to the operator Lisa Jefferson instead. Jefferson called the FBI on another line and asked Beamer numerous questions, relaying his answers to the FBI. How many hijackers were there?

David, Andrew, and Lisa Beamer pose with the picture of husband and father Todd, one of the Flight 93 passengers who attempted to overcome their hijackers.

Were they armed? What did they want? Beamer provided the answers as best he could, sometimes asking another passenger before making his response. This provided crucial information to the FBI in investigating the case later.

Toward the end of the phone call, Beamer began to talk about his family. He talked of his wife, his sons, and the new baby on the way. He asked Jefferson to tell his family that he loved them.

A devout Christian, Beamer asked Jefferson to recite the Lord's Prayer with him. After that, he began to recite the twenty-third Psalm from the Bible. Jefferson could hear other passengers join in as they recited the Psalm along with Beamer. "Though I walk through the valley of the shadow of death," they recited, "I will fear no evil."

Finally, Beamer told Jefferson that the passengers were planning to attack the hijackers. As Jefferson remained on the phone, Beamer began talking seriously with the other passengers as they planned their strategy. The last words she heard from him were, "Are you guys ready? OK. Let's roll!"

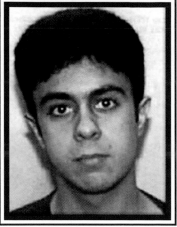

Photos of suspected Flight 93 hijackers Ahmed Alnami *(top left)*, Saeed Alghamdi *(top center)*, Ziad Jarrah *(top right)*, and Ahmed Al Haznawi *(bottom left)*, released by the U.S. Department of Justice during its investigation of the crash of Flight 93.

hijackings before the horrific events of September 11 took place, they needed to attempt to overtake the terrorists. Some passengers were more prepared than others to attack the hijackers. This was, after all, going against federal emergency regulations and the caution exercised in prior hijackings. There was a huge risk involved, and at least one woman on the ground told her husband on his cell phone to just sit back, be quiet, and obey the hijackers' demands.

So, in true American fashion, the passengers decided to take a vote. Would they sit back and comply with the hijackers' demands, the course of action that until now had been the safest response for passengers and crew members involved in an airplane hijacking? This, after all,

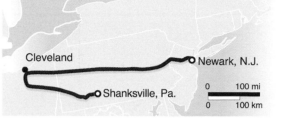

United Airlines 93:
Crashed in rural southwest Pennsylvania

From Newark, N.J., to San Francisco – 45 people on board

Here is a partial list of those killed in Tuesday's terrorist attacks, according to family members, friends, co-workers and law enforcement.

CREW:
Jason Dahl, Denver, captain
Leroy Homer, Marlton, N.J., first officer
Lorraine Bay, flight attendant
Sandra Bradshaw, 38, Greensboro, N.C., flight attendant
Wanda Green, flight attendant
CeeCee Lyles, Fort Myers, Fla., flight attendant
Deborah Welsh, flight attendant

PASSENGERS:
Christian Adams
Todd Beamer
Alan Beaven, 48, San Francisco,

environmental lawyer
Mark Bingham, 31, San Francisco, public relations executive
Deora Bodley, 20, Santa Clara, university student
Marion Britton
Thomas E. Burnett Jr., 38, San Ramon, Calif., senior vice president and chief operating officer, Thoratec Corp.
William Cashman
Georgine Corrigan
Joseph Deluca
Patrick Driscoll
Edward Felt, 41, Matawan, N.J.
Colleen Fraser

Andrew Garcia
Jeremy Glick
Lauren Grandcolas, San Rafael, Calif., sales worker at Good Housekeeping magazine
Donald F. Greene, 52, Greenwich, Conn.
Linda Gronlund
Richard Guadagno, 38, northern California
Toshiya Kuge
Waleska Martinez
Nicole Miller
Mark Rothenberg
Christine Snyder, 32, Kailua, Hawaii
John Talignani
Honor Wainio

SOURCE: Compiled from AP wire Reports

AP

Associated Press information about the crash of Flight 93—posted online days after the crash—showed the plane's route and all known passengers and crew members killed. On September 11, many news Web sites experienced a high volume of Internet traffic as people all over the world sought information about the terrorist attacks.

was what the federal emergency regulations and airline safety procedures advised.

Or would they attack the hijackers, going against the formally prescribed rules? Would they attempt to overtake the terrorists and regain control of the airplane in hopes that they could save their own lives, or at least the lives of many other innocent people on the ground?

No one knows how each passenger voted, or how many votes there were for each side. One would like to believe that the vote was unanimous. In any case, the result of the vote was clear: The passengers had no other choice. They would attack the hijackers.

In March of 2002, the U.S. Air Force unveiled a new emblem featuring the words "Let's Roll!" as a tribute to Todd Beamer and other Flight 93 passengers.

"LET'S ROLL!"

CHAPTER

O nce the vote had been taken, there was nothing more to do but go for it. The passengers and flight attendants had already discussed a variety of plans among themselves, and one can assume that they had come to know each other well enough in the short amount of time that they had to understand each other's strengths and weaknesses.

The passengers must have seen the flight attendants filling up coffeepots with boiling water, and the flight attendants must have heard those passengers trained in combat or martial arts discussing their skills. The business executives, or those with organizational skills, may have formulated a strategy and given each person a specific task. Because they were calm enough to discuss the situation and take a vote among themselves, they most likely would have been able to come up with a grand plan that all of them would follow.

"Let's roll!" is a common American slang phrase that is often heard in action and adventure movies. These are the words of a military team ready to attack a target, or the exclamation expressed by a group of police officers preparing to capture a criminal. They were also the last words heard spoken to telephone operator Lisa Jefferson by passenger Todd Beamer. These were the only words required to get the passengers moving in their desperate attempt to overtake their captors.

Coffee Pots and Commandos

One of the flight attendants had told her husband that she and others were filling coffeepots with boiling water to throw at the terrorists. The group of martial arts experts, athletes, and former law enforcement officers formed a team of makeshift commandos. They had spoken with their loved ones and had taken a vote. They were ready. At the sound of those famous last words, "Let's roll," the passengers began running over 100 feet to the front of the airplane to break into the cockpit.

A few of the passengers were still on the telephone with their loved ones when the action began. "I need to go," said the disabled activist to her stepmother. "They're getting

CeeCee Lyles *(left)* and Wanda Anita Green were two of the flight attendants aboard Flight 93. They and other attendants may have helped overcome the hijackers.

ready to break into the cockpit. I love you. Goodbye." The thirty-seven-year United Airlines veteran told her husband, "Everyone's running to first class. I've got to go. 'Bye." Another flight attendant simply screamed, "They're doing it! They're doing it! They're doing it!" And the judo champion told his family, in classic Arnold Schwarzenegger style, "I'll be back."

From the last words spoken to their families, it appears that all or most of the passengers and crew of the plane were involved in the fight with the terrorists. Final statements like "I've got to go" and "I'll be back" indicated that these passengers intended on helping in whatever way they could. Certainly, the passengers hoped to save their own lives as well as the lives of others on the ground. And, after hearing the last words that they spoke to their families, it appears that they truly believed they had a chance of doing just that.

A Fight for Their Lives

No one knows, nor will we ever know, who did what or exactly what happened next. The judo expert may have used his expertise to take out one or more of the terrorists. The disabled activist may have used her cane to trip or hit a hijacker. The flight attendants may have thrown boiling water on the terrorists, as planned. The large rugby player or the former football player may have struggled with the hijackers or pulled them from the cockpit of the airplane while the aircraft experts attempted to gain the airplane's controls. All we know for certain is that the passengers were in a fight for their lives.

After running 100 feet to the front of the airplane, the passengers broke into the cockpit and began to battle with the terrorists. A violent scuffle ensued, as the passengers tried to subdue the hijackers and regain control of the airplane. The airplane bobbed up and down, flying erratically as the passengers and terrorists each scrambled to gain control. "Give it to me!" was later heard on the cockpit voice recorder, apparently shouted by a hijacker attempting to grab the airplane's controls.

Local residents and air traffic controllers watched from the ground as the gigantic commercial jet airplane

At a news conference on September 19, 2001, Lee Purbaugh describes watching Flight 93 crash into a field outside of Shanksville, Pennsylvania.

soared through the skies above them in a frighteningly unstable manner. The plane bobbed up and down and from side to side as though the pilot had completely lost control. They watched as the plane came closer and closer to the ground, and several local air traffic controllers evacuated their tower for fear that the plane would crash into it. They could have had no idea what was going on in that giant airplane in the sky above them.

A Loud Crash

Suddenly, a loud crash was heard by residents of Shanksville, Pennsylvania, and all over the surrounding area. The crash

An aerial view of the Flight 93 crash site, taken by the FBI on September 19, 2001

was heard for miles. Residents in the area said that their houses shook, their windows rattled, and that it felt like a huge earthquake or tornado had hit their little town.

Five days after the crash of Flight 93, FBI investigators were still excavating the field and gathering important data.

Tragically, the passengers and crew of United Airlines Flight 93 were unable to subdue the terrorists and regain control of the airplane before it crashed into a wooded field in Somerset County, Pennsylvania, about 80 miles southeast of Pittsburgh. All of the passengers and crew of that flight who had not already been killed by the terrorists, as well as the terrorists who had hijacked the airplane, died in the crash. The heroes who fought to stop the terrorists from carrying out their evil plan gave their lives for many other innocent victims who may have died that day had the plane been flown into its target destination. They most likely also saved one of America's precious landmarks and retained hope until the very end of saving their own lives as well. They were true heroes.

After the crash, the site was fenced off by the FBI so that the plane's flight data recorder, also known as the "black box," and its cockpit voice recorder could be recovered. The

A LARGE CRATER

Acommercial jet airplane the size of Flight 93, carrying enough fuel to take it across the United States, would create nothing but a huge fiery crater if it crashed into the ground. And that is exactly what this plane did.

According to one observer at the site who is quoted on http://www.flight93.org, "Everything was on fire and there were trees knocked down and there was a big hole in the ground." The plane crashed into a large, grassy field surrounded by woods, creating a V-shaped crater about 8 to10 feet deep and15 to 20 feet long. According to the FBI, the crater will be filled in when all of the debris at the sight has been recovered and no further analysis at the site is necessary. Many want to turn the site into a memorial, honoring those who stood up to the terrorists who were most likely trying to attack our nation's capital.

By the time you read this book, a memorial may already have been erected for visitors and loved ones to mourn the dead heroes. Someday you may be able to visit the site where the plane crashed and see for yourself the damage that the crash caused. For more information on this, check the official Flight 93 memorial site at http://www.flt93memorial.org/.

FBI also wanted to salvage as much as possible of the doomed plane, including the passengers' bodies and their belongings, and any other information that might assist them in their investigation. Within a few days, the plane's black box was found, and soon after the cockpit voice recorder was found as well. The analysis of these recorders, along with the analysis of the debris located at the crash site, coupled with interviews with the family members and friends of passengers who had had conversations with their loved ones, provided important evidence to the FBI in its investigation of this case.

Organizers of a September 11 anniversary memorial answer questions at a news conference in July of 2002.

DISASTER AVERTED

The crash of United Airlines Flight 93 was indeed a terrible tragedy. All of the passengers and crew on board the flight were killed, and they left behind many loved ones who cared for them and mourned them deeply. The passengers who embarked on their quest to save the doomed flight were unsuccessful in their attempt to save their own lives.

However, due to the heroics of the passengers and crew on board the flight, a far more horrible disaster that may have occurred was prevented. Many, many more innocent people may have been killed had the passengers and crew of United Airlines Flight 93 not braved the horror that was before them. Had they voted to remain seated and be quiet, the plane may have crashed into one of the nation's major monuments, and may very well have taken the lives of hundreds or even thousands of others. In this respect, because of the bravery of those on United Airlines Flight 93, a far more terrible disaster was averted.

The Intended Target

It is not known for certain, and it may never be known, where the terrorists who hijacked United Airlines Flight 93 intended to crash the airplane. The FBI and other investigators have concluded that there were three likely targets: Camp David, the presidential retreat; the White House; and the Capitol building in Washington, D.C.

Of the three targets, Camp David is the least likely, according to the evidence gathered. Camp David is the place where the president goes when he needs a rest. Just after gaining control of the airplane, one of the terrorists asked air traffic control for a new flight plan—to Washington, D.C. Camp David is located in Maryland. In addition, the terrorists could not have known whether the president was staying at Camp David at the time, and in fact he was not. In the terrorists' eyes, Camp David would have been a less advantageous target, since the president is not there often and since there were not a large number of other government

The White House in Washington, D.C., was briefly evacuated during the terrorist attacks on September 11, 2001. Later information obtained by the U.S. government indicates that it may have been the intended target for the hijackers of Flight 93.

officials located at this site. Therefore, although we do not know for certain, many investigators of the crash assume that Camp David was not the intended target.

The White House, where the president of the United States, vice president, and his many invaluable cabinet members conduct most of their business, is a far more likely target than Camp David. It would have been a far better target in the minds of the terrorists. Either the president or the vice president, or both, would likely be there on that morning, and there are numerous aides and cabinet members, upon whom the president relies for information and important advice, who would certainly have been there at the time. Also, since the White House is located in Washington, D.C., where the terrorists had requested to fly, it makes sense that the terrorists may have intended to crash the plane into the White House.

The Capitol building, also located in Washington, D.C., is another very likely target. The Capitol building, where our senators and representatives conduct their meetings and make laws, is a structure that reminds many Americans of the democratic principles of their nation. Many Americans regard the Capitol building as the place in Washington where our elected officials represent us. Had there been a meeting among the Senate or the House of Representatives, or both, that morning, many of our elected officials might have been killed, placing a deep wound in the heart of America.

New evidence gathered in May 2002 suggests that the White House was the intended target. Government officials announced that a captured terrorist had provided them with this information; therefore it may or may not be accurate. Although we may never know the intended target of the terrorists, we can only assume it was one that could have caused great damage to America and would have killed many, many innocent people. Thanks to the heroes on United Airlines Flight 93, this did not happen.

The Shoot-down Theory

Soon after September 11, several U.S. and foreign news sources reported that a U.S. military fighter jet shot down

All the events listed in the timeline below occurred on the morning of September 11, 2001. Due to the uncertain nature of the events, this timeline is approximate. Times were provided by reports from ABCNews.com, CNN, and *Newsweek*.

7:58 AM   United Airlines Flight 175 departs Boston's Logan airport.

7:59 AM   American Airlines Flight 11 departs Boston's Logan airport.

8:01 AM   United Airlines Flight 93 is scheduled to depart New Jersey's Newark International airport.

8:10 AM   American Airlines Flight 77 departs Washington Dulles airport.

8:42 AM   United Airlines Flight 93 departs Newark International airport.

8:45 AM   American Airlines Flight 11 crashes into the first tower of the World Trade Center in New York City.

9:02 AM   A message flashes on the cockpit's computer screen of United Airlines Flight 93: "Beware, cockpit intrusion." The message is confirmed by one of the pilots.

9:06 AM   United Airlines Flight 175 hits the second tower of the World Trade Center.

9:25 AM   The terrorists on United Airlines Flight 93 tie red bandannas around their heads.

9:26 AM   Voices are heard in the cockpit of United Airlines Flight 93— "Get out of here! Get out of here!"

9:31 AM   The passengers on United Airlines Flight 93 begin making telephone calls to their friends and family members.

9:38 AM   A thickly accented voice is heard at air traffic control in Cleveland, Ohio, saying "This is the captain speaking . . . There is a bomb on board . . ."

9:40 AM   American Airlines Flight 77 crashes into the Pentagon.

9:53 AM   A vote is taken among the passengers of United Airlines Flight 93, resulting in the decision to attack the terrorists. The telephone calls between the passengers and their loved ones end.

9:54 AM   United Airlines Flight 93 begins to fly erratically, soaring closer and closer to the ground.

9:57 AM   Sounds of a struggle in the cockpit of United Airlines Flight 93 are heard.

10:06 AM   United Airlines Flight 93 crashes in a field in Somerset County, Pennsylvania.

Secretary of Defense Donald Rumsfeld gives a speech at the Pentagon one day before the terrorist attacks. Ironically, his speech emphasized cutting military spending and even eliminating some jobs in the military services.

United Airlines Flight 93 before it was able to reach its intended destination. If this were true, numerous questions would need to be addressed: Were the passengers of United Airlines Flight 93 actually the heroes described, or were they merely victims? Could the passengers actually have saved their own lives and landed the plane safely had the plane not been shot down? Should the U.S. military shoot down hijacked airplanes?

Many people struggled with these questions as the news reports came out. There were reports by witnesses on the ground in Pennsylvania that a large bang was heard before the crash, and that a U.S. fighter jet sped over the site just after the crash occurred. Other news reports suggested that a U.S. Air Force fighter jet was on

THIS MEMORIAL IS IN MEMORY
OF THE BRAVE MEN AND WOMEN
WHO GAVE THEIR LIVES
TO SAVE SO MANY OTHERS.
THEIR COURAGE AND LOVE
OF OUR COUNTRY WILL BE
A SOURCE OF STRENGTH AND COMFORT
TO OUR GREAT NATION.
GOD BLESS AMERICA.

CHRISTIAN ADAMS
FLIGHT ATTENDANT LORRAINE G. BAY
TODD BEAMER
ALAN BEAVEN
MARK BINGHAM
DEORA BODLEY
FLIGHT ATTENDANT SANDRA W. BRADSHAW
MARION BRITTON
THOMAS BURNETT
WILLIAM CASHMAN
GEORGINE CORRIGAN
PATRICIA CUSHING
CAPTAIN JASON DAHL
JOSEPH DELUCA
PATRICK DRISCOLL
EDWARD FELT
JANE C. FOLGER
COLLEEN FRASER
ANDREW GARCIA
JEREMY GLICK
KRISTIN GOULD
LAUREN GRANDCOLAS
FLIGHT ATTENDANT WANDA A. GREEN
DONALD GREENE
LINDA GRONLUND
RICHARD GUADAGNO
FIRST OFFICER LEROY HOMER
TOSHIYA KUGE
FLIGHT ATTENDANT CEECEE LYLES
HILDA MARCIN
WALESKA MARTINEZ
NICOLE MILLER
LOUIS J. NACKE
DONALD PETERSON
JEAN PETERSON
MARK ROTHENBERG
CHRISTINE SNYDER
JOHN TALIGNANI
HONOR ELIZABETH WAINIO
FLIGHT ATTENDANT DEBORAH A. WELSH

UNITED FLIGHT 93
SEPTEMBER 11, 2001

A plaque honoring all the passengers and crew members who died in the crash of United Airlines Flight 93 was dedicated outside Shanksville, Pennsylvania, on March 11, 2002.

its way but didn't arrive in time to shoot down United Airlines Flight 93. Residents in the area also described burning wreckage falling from the sky, suggesting that the plane had exploded before hitting the ground.

However, almost immediately after these reports appeared in the press, Pentagon officials firmly denied that United Airlines Flight 93 was shot down by a military fighter jet. U.S. Department of Defense secretary Donald Rumsfeld told Diane Sawyer in an ABC news interview, "The idea of the United States military going up and shooting down an American airline plane filled with American citizens is not something one contemplates." Several days later, the FBI, conducting its own investigation of the shoot-down theory, confirmed that there was no bomb residue or evidence of any explosives at the crash site. Furthermore, there were no reports of an explosion on the plane's cockpit voice recorder, which would certainly have occurred had the plane been shot down. We can only conclude, therefore, that the rumors that United Airlines Flight 93 had been shot down were just that: rumors and nothing else.

The First Soldiers in the War Against Terrorism

After the four planes were hijacked on September 11 and crashed by terrorists into various locations in the United States, President George W. Bush declared a "war on terror." The U.S. Department of Defense geared up for an attempt to determine who was responsible for these horrible crimes,

A 1999 photo of Afghan soldiers who opposed the Taliban camped outside of Kabul, Afghanistan. After the attacks on September 11, 2001, the United States attacked Afghan targets in an attempt to catch Al Qaeda members.

and to eliminate their evil operations. Osama bin Laden is believed to be the mastermind behind the operation, and his network of terrorists, Al Qaeda, the ones who carried out these terrible deeds.

It was determined that Osama bin Laden and the headquarters of his terrorist network were located in Afghanistan, a country in south central Asia, south of Russia and west of China. The United States asked the acting government (though not the official government) of Afghanistan, the Taliban, to help them locate and punish this network of terror. But because the Taliban refused to help the

A temporary memorial set up near the crash site in May of 2002, dedicated to the passengers and crew members who died on Flight 93.

United States, and instead were believed to be involved in assisting the terrorists in carrying out their plans, the United States led an all-out war on the Taliban. The United States was helped by England, Canada, and several other democratic countries.

Eventually, the Taliban was removed from power and many members of Al Qaeda were captured. A new government was established in Afghanistan, a government that would not allow terrorist activities or organizations to operate in their land. This was how the war on terror, in many people's eyes, began.

However, the first true soldiers in the war against terrorism were those passengers and crew on United Airlines Flight 93, who, going against rules that stated that passengers and crew should obey hijackers' demands, fought and won at least part of their battle. Although they were unable to save themselves, they saved the lives of countless others on the ground who might otherwise have been killed on that fateful day. The passengers and crew of United Airlines Flight 93, who so courageously fought for their own lives and for the lives of others, should truly be regarded as the first soldiers in the war against terrorism.

GLOSSARY

Airphone   A telephone located on the backs of seats in most commercial jet airplanes.

black box   An airplane's flight data recorder, which records details such as where the plane was located when it crashed, how fast the plane was flying, and other important data. It is made of material designed to withstand the most destructive crashes or fires.

cockpit   The area in an airplane where a pilot and copilot fly the plane.

hijacker   Someone who takes over an airplane by force, usually with weapons or a bomb, and usually directs the plane to a location other than the one originally intended.

Islam   A religion whose God is called Allah and which is practiced by millions of people throughout the world.

jihad   A concept of Islam meaning "to struggle," usually referring to the struggle one makes to become a better person.

Pentagon   The building in Arlington, Virginia, where America's defense and military actions are led. It is called the Pentagon because of its unique architecture, which consists of five sides, resembling the geometric shape of the same name.

terrorist   An individual who attacks or harms innocent people, usually in the attempt to gain his or her political or religious goals.

For More Information

Federal Bureau of Investigation (FBI)
Department of Justice
935 Pennsylvania Avenue, NW
Room 7972
Washington, DC 20535
(202) 324-3000
Web site: http://www.fbi.gov/

Federal Emergency Management Agency (FEMA)
500 C Street, SW
Washington, DC 20472
(202) 566-1600
Web site: http://www.fema.gov

U.S. Department of Defense
1400 Defense Pentagon, Room 3A750
Washington, DC 20301-1400
(703) 428-0711
Web site: http://www.defenselink.mil

U.S. Department of Justice
950 Pennsylvania Avenue, NW
Washington, DC 20530-0001
(202) 353-1555
Web site: http://www.usdoj.gov

U.S. Department of State
2201 C Street, NW
Washington, DC 20520
(202) 647-4000
Web site: http://www.state.gov

Web Sites

Due to the changing nature of Internet links, the Rosen Publishing Group, Inc., has developed an online list of Web sites related to the subject of this book. This site is updated regularly. Please use this link to access the list:

http://www.rosenlinks.com/ta/cuf9/

FOR FURTHER READING

Bishop, Jennifer. *Through the Eyes of Freedom: A Teen Perspective on September 11, 2001*. Oklahoma City, OK: New Horizons Publishing, 2002.

Gordon, Matthew S. *Islam.* New York: Facts on File, Inc., 1991.

Heuvel, Katrina Vanden. *A Just Response: The Nation on Terrorism, Democracy, and September 11, 2001*. New York: Thunder's Mouth Press, 2002.

Marsh, Carole. *United We Stand: America's War Against Terrorism*. Atlanta, GA: Gallopade Publishing Group, 2001.

Wells, Donna Koren, and Bruce C. Morris. *Live Aware, Not in Fear: The 411 on 9-11*. Deerfield Beach, FL: Health Communications, 2002.

Wheeler, Jill C. *September 11, 2001: The Day That Changed America*. Edina, MN: Abdo & Daughters, 2002.

Zacharias, Ravi K. *Light in the Shadow of Jihad*. Sisters, OR: Multnomah Publishers Inc., 2002.

BIBLIOGRAPHY

Barker, Kim, Louise Kiernan, and Steve Mills. "The Heroes of Flight 93: Interviews with Family and Friends Detail the Courage of Everyday People." *Chicago Tribune.* October 2, 2001.

Breslau, Karen. "The Final Moments of United Flight 93." *Newsweek.* September 22, 2001.

Breslau, Karen. "Reporting on United Flight 93." *Newsweek.* November 26, 2001.

Breslau, Karen, Eleanor Clift, and Evan Thomas. "The Real Story of Flight 93." *Newsweek.* December 3, 2001.

Dizikes, Peter. ABCNews.com. "The Mystery of Flight 93," September 13, 2001. Retrieved April 2002 (http://www.abcnews.com).

Dizikes, Peter. ABCNews.com. "What Happened to Flight 93?" September 12, 2001. Retrieved April 2002 (http://www.abcnews.com).

Guardian Unlimited. "Alleged hijacker's emails to flight school published." February 8, 2002. Retrieved October 8, 2002 (http://www.guardian.co.uk/september11/story/0,11209,647313,00.html).

Isikoff, Michael, and Daniel Klaidman. "A Matter of Missed Signals." *Newsweek*. December 24, 2001.

Johnson, Kevin, and Alan Levin. "Recorder Catchers Passengers' Fight with Hijackers." *USA Today*. October 3, 2001.

Lumpkin, John J. "White House Was Target of Flight 93." Associated Press. May 23, 2002.

Morgan, David. "Flight Data Recorder Found at Pennsylvania Crash Site." Reuters News Service. September 13, 2001.

Vulliamy, Ed. "Let's Roll. . . ." *The Observer*. December 2, 2001.

INDEX

About the Author

Tonya Buell is a writer in Mesa, Arizona. She was deeply affected by the September 11, 2001 terrorist attacks and since September 11 she has been spending more and more time with her friends and family members. This is her third book.

Photo Credits

Cover, pp. 6–7, 8, 13, 14–15, 17, 21, 28, 31, 33, 34–35, 37, 39–42, 44–45, 47, 50, 51, 53, 54 © AP/Wide World Photos; p. 5 © Corbis; pp. 24–25 © Reuters NewMedia Inc./Corbis; p. 32 © AFP/Corbis.

Editor

Christine Poolos

Series Design and Layout

Geri Giordano